Community Workers

Caring For Your Pets

A Book About Veterinarians

Ann Owen

Illustrated by Eric Thomas

Thanks to our advisers for their expertise, research, knowledge, and advice:

Jennifer Zablotny, D.V.M., Lansing, Michigan

Susan Kesselring, M.A., Literacy Educator
Rosemount-Apple Valley-Eagan (Minnesota) School District

PICTURE WINDOW BOOKS
Minneapolis, Minnesota

Managing Editor: Bob Temple
Creative Director: Terri Foley
Editor: Peggy Henrikson
Editorial Adviser: Andrea Cascardi
Copy Editor: Laurie Kahn
Designer: John Moldstad
Page production: Picture Window Books
The illustrations in this book were prepared digitally.

Picture Window Books
1710 Roe Crest Drive
North Mankato, MN 56003
877-845-8392
www.capstonepub.com

Library of Congress Cataloging-in-Publication Data
Owen, Ann, 1953–
Caring for your pets : a book about veterinarians / by Ann Owen ; illustrated by Eric Thomas.
p. cm. — (Community workers)
Includes bibliographical references.
Summary: Describes some of the things that veterinarians do to help animals stay healthy.
ISBN-13: 978-1-4048-0087-8 (hardcover)
ISBN-10: 1-4048-0087-5 (hardcover)
ISBN-13: 978-1-4048-0481-4 (paperback)
ISBN-10: 1-4048-0481-1 (paperback)
1. Veterinarians—Juvenile literature. 2. Veterinary medicine—Vocational guidance—Juvenile literature.
[1. Veterinarians. 2. Veterinary medicine. 3. Occupations.]
I. Thomas, Eric, ill. II. Title. III. Community workers (Picture Window Books)
SF756 .O94 2004
636.089'092—dc21
                                                                        2003004167

Many people in your community have jobs helping others. Veterinarians are doctors for animals. They care for people's pets. Veterinarians are often called vets.

What does a veterinarian do?

The veterinarian helps your pet.
If your pet is sick or hurt, a vet will help.

I don't think Rusty feels well.

Vets help big pets and small ones.

The vet asks you what your pet is like.

Bud loves to run.

You tell the vet what your
pet eats, when it sleeps,
and if it likes to play.

The vet listens to your pet's heart and lungs.

Stay, Boots!
That's a good girl.

The vet checks
your pet's eyes,

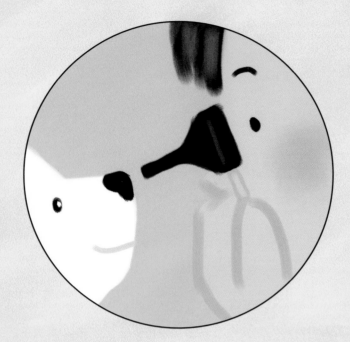

looks in its ears,

and checks
its teeth.

The vet checks your pet's fur and paws.

Slinky looks great.
I can tell you take very
good care of him.

The vet tells you what medicine to give

and how to give it.

Sometimes, the vet needs
to give your pet a shot.

That wasn't bad,
was it, Cookie?

The vet will explain what to feed your pet.

Some vets visit farms. These vets take care of bigger animals, such as horses, cows, and pigs.

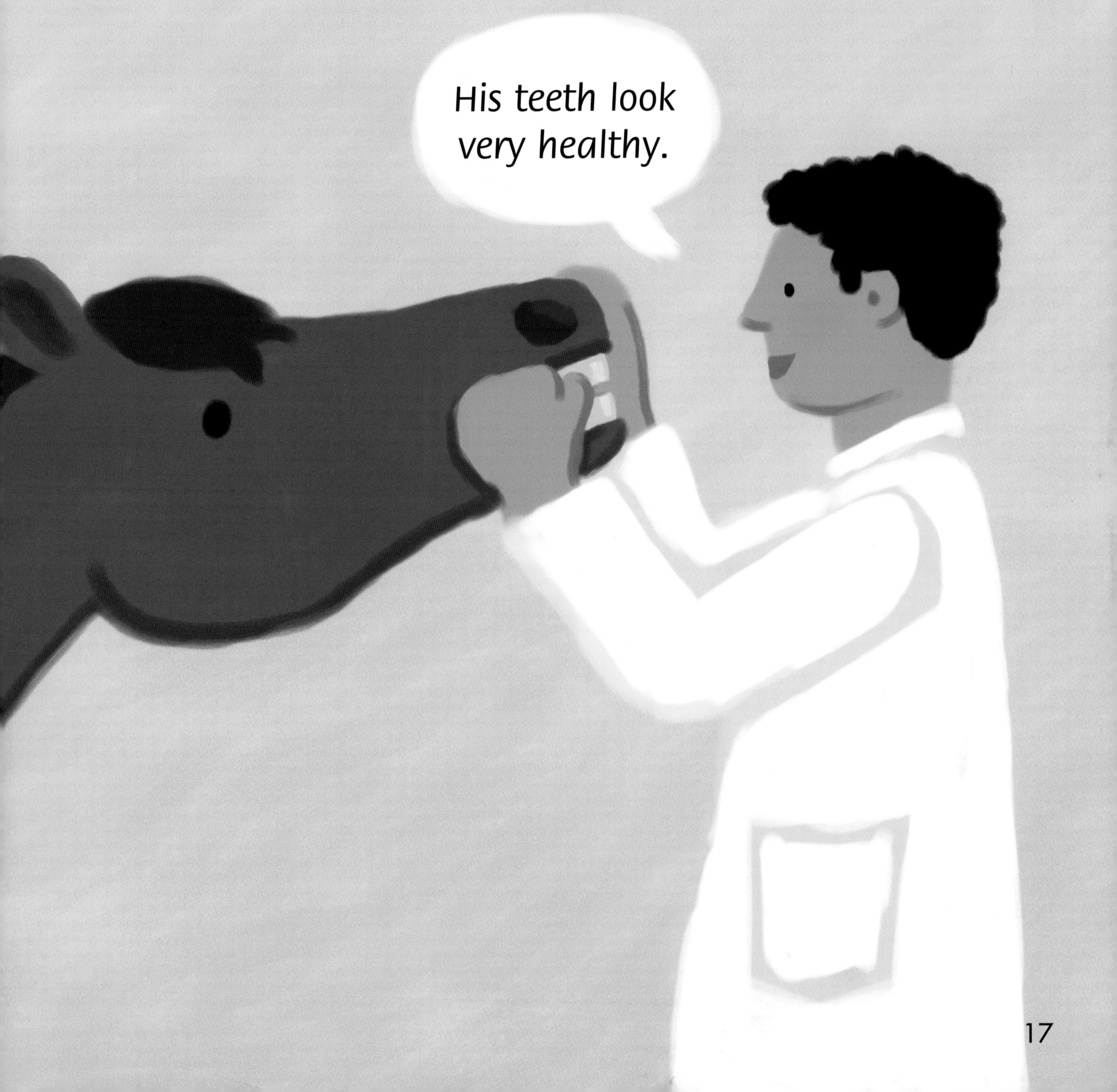
His teeth look very healthy.

Some vets work in zoos.

Some vets help wild animals
that have been hurt.

Veterinarians care for your pets.

Did You Know?

A vet's work can be dangerous. A farm vet has to be extra careful to keep from being kicked or bitten by a frightened animal. A zoo vet gives wild animals special shots to make them sleep during the vet's exam.

Most vets work in offices or animal hospitals. Some work at animal shelters, zoos, or labs. A farm vet may work out of a truck that carries the vet's supplies. Vets who work with wild animals may work outdoors. Some vets even work at racetracks.

To become a vet, a person has to have four years of veterinary college after regular college. Today there are more women in veterinary school than men.

Ancient records show that Egyptians were giving medical treatment to cattle, dogs, birds, and fish about 3,800 years ago.

When Should Your Pet See the Vet?

A sick pet acts a lot like you when you're sick. Sometimes it's easy to know when to take your pet to see the vet. Sometimes it's not.

Take your pet to the vet if your pet ...

- coughs or throws up a lot,

- seems especially tired,

- isn't eating the same foods or the same amount that it usually does,

- has eaten something bad,

- is limping or moving differently, or

- is due for a regular checkup. Even if your pet is not sick, the vet will still want to make sure that everything is okay. Ask your vet how often you should bring in your pet for a checkup.

Can you think of other times to take your pet to the vet?

Words to Know

animal hospital (AN-uh-muhl HOSS-pi-tuhl) — a building where vets and others work to help animals who are very sick or badly hurt

animal shelter (AN-uh-muhl SHEL-tur) — a place that takes care of unwanted animals

community (kuh-MYOO-nuh-tee) — a group of people who live in the same area

lab (LAB) — a place for scientific experiments. Lab is short for laboratory.

medicine (MED-uh-suhn) — a substance used to help sick or injured animals (or people) get better

veterinarian (vet-ur-uh-NAIR-ee-uhn) — a doctor for animals

veterinary (VET-ur-uh-nair-ee) — having to do with the treatment of animals

23

To Learn More

At the Library

Grace, Catherine O'Neill. *I Want to Be a Veterinarian*. San Diego: Harcourt Brace, 1997.

Greene, Carol. *Veterinarians Help Animals*. Plymouth, Minn.: Child's World, 1997.

Horenstein, Henry. *My Mom's a Vet*. Cambridge, Mass.: Candlewick Press, 1994.

Ready, Dee. *Veterinarians*. Mankato, Minn.: Bridgestone Books, 1997.

Schaefer, Lola M. *We Need Veterinarians*. Mankato, Minn.: Pebble Books, 2000.

On the Web

American Animal Hospital Association
For information on pet care and for pet pages to color
http://www.healthypet.com

American Veterinary Medical Association: Care for Animals
For fun activities and information on caring for animals
http://www.avma.org/careforanimals

Fact Hound
Want more information about veterinarians and animals?
Fact Hound offers a safe, fun way to find Web sites related to this book.
All of the sites on Fact Hound have been researched by our staff.
http://www.facthound.com

1. Visit the Fact Hound home page.
2. Enter a search word related to this book,
   or type in this special code: 1404800875.
3. Click on the FETCH IT button.

Your trusty Fact Hound will fetch the best sites for you!

Index

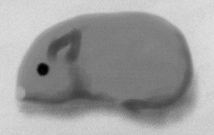